No Limits

IN-LINE SKATING

Jed Morgan

A⁺

Smart Apple Media

First published in 2005 by Franklin Watts
96 Leonard Street, London EC2A 4XD

Franklin Watts Australia
45–51 Huntley Street, Alexandria NSW 2015

Series editor: Adrian Cole, Series design: Pewter Design Associates, Art director: Jonathan Hair, Picture researcher: Sophie Hartley

Acknowledgements:
The publisher acknowledges all © products shown within this title as the property of their respective owners. Steve Bardens/Action Plus: 5t, 8b. DPPI/Action Plus: 27b. Courtesy www.citiskate.co.uk: 19t. Courtesy K2 (UK) Limited: 4bl, 7t & b, 9l, tr & br, 10t, 11tl, 12t, 16t, 26. Photo by Frank Manischewski: 19b. National Museum of Roller Skating, Lincoln, Nebraska: 4t. © Stephen Olner: 18. © Andrew Padden: 29 (inset). © Pari-Roller: 11tr, 16b. AGF/Rex Features: 27t. Alisdair Macdonald/Rex Features: 15b. Courtesy Rollerblade International:4br, 5b, 6-7, 8t, 9cr, 10b, 20r, 21b, 22b, 23t, 25b. © SCC-Running: 17b. © Stockfile/Steven Behr: 11b, 12b, 13t & b, 14t, 15t, 20l, 21tl, tc & tr, 22t, 23bl & br, 24t, 25tl, tc & tr. © Stockfile/Jess Dyrenforth: 24b, 28, 29 (main). © Superstock: Cover, 14b. Courtesy Zephyr Adventures www.zephyradventures.com: 17t.

Published in the United States by Smart Apple Media
2140 Howard Drive West, North Mankato, Minnesota 56003

Library of Congress Cataloging-in-Publication Data

Morgan, Jed.
In-line skating / by Jed Morgan.
p. cm. — (No limits)
Originally published: London : Franklin Watts, 2005.
Includes index.
ISBN-13 : 978-1-58340-957-2
1. In-line skating—Juvenile literature. I. Title.

GV859.73.M67 2006
796.21—dc22   2005052564

9 8 7 6 5 4 3 2 1

Important Note:

Disclaimer—In the preparation of this book, all due care has been exercised with regard to the activities depicted. The publishers regret that they can accept no liability for any loss or injury sustained.

Contents

World of in-line skating

In-line skates allow you to reach mind-boggling speeds, perform amazing tricks, or just cruise around the park. They give you incredible freedom to explore the world around you.

Early in-line skating

A Belgian named Joseph Merlin developed the earliest-known in-line skates in 1760 to practice ice-skating on dry land. By 1819, M. Petitbled of France patented a three-wheeled version, and an English skate called the "Rolito" followed in 1823. Forty years later, a new roller skate with two parallel sets of wheels changed everything. Roller skates were easier to use, and in-line skating went out of style.

The "Petitbled" had three rubber wheels mounted in a line on a wooden frame.

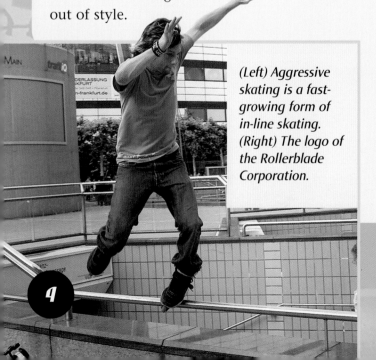

(Left) Aggressive skating is a fast-growing form of in-line skating. (Right) The logo of the Rollerblade Corporation.

In-line reborn

Modern in-line skates can be traced back to 1979. Two hockey players, Scott and Brennan Olson from Minneapolis, Minnesota, experimented with an old in-line skate. In 1980, they started a company to produce an in-line skate they called a "Rollerblade." By 1984, they had sold their company. An improved version of their Rollerblade, called "Lightning TRS," became the first truly popular in-line skate.

ROLLERBLADE

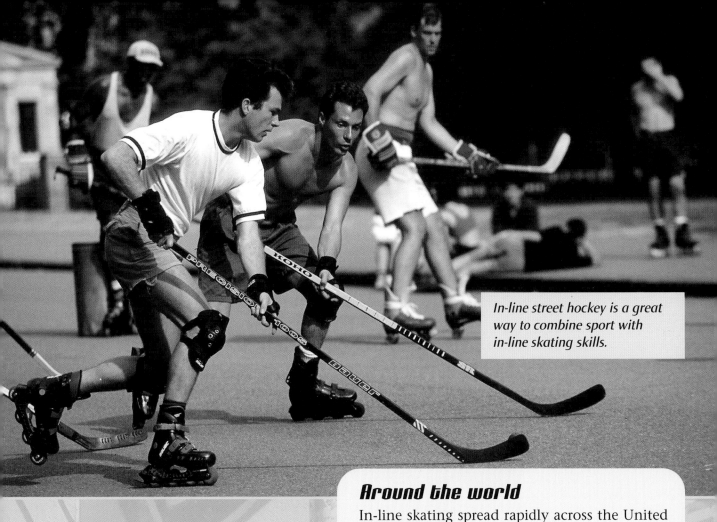

In-line street hockey is a great way to combine sport with in-line skating skills.

FROM THE EDGE

"All in-line skaters are united by a common experience: the thrill and easy feeling of having seemingly frictionless wheels on their feet, and the freedom of movement, expression, and speed in-line skating lets them achieve." Michael Zaidman, Director and Curator of the National Museum of Roller Skating (1996–99), Lincoln, Nebraska. The museum collects, preserves, and researches everything to do with in-line and roller skating history.

Around the world

In-line skating spread rapidly across the United States. By the end of the 1990s, there were more than 32 million in-line skaters in the U.S. alone—more than the entire population of Scandinavia! As the design improved further, in-line skates were marketed for exercise or racing and for the fast-growing sport of in-line hockey. By 1997, in-line skating had become a billion-dollar worldwide sport, and it's still growing today.

Know your skates

In-line skates look similar, but there are many different types. This Rollerblade Lightning 05 is a high-performance skate, but it has many features in common with other skates.

Liner — PFS PROfessional LITE with Coolmax© technology

SHELL (outer boot that gives the skate its shape)
* Design — Most shells are made of types of plastic, including ballistic nylon. Often, plastic is combined with other materials, such as carbon fiber, to provide more flexibility. Such shells are called composite shells.
* Air vents — Increase airflow in the boot.
* Cuff — Helps transfer power from your leg to the skate.

BRAKE
Recreational in-line skates are fitted with a brake. The brake is usually on the heel of the right-hand skate. It consists of a brake support and replaceable rubber pad.

Shell — Fiberglass-charged plastic with Soft Touch© finish

WHEEL FRAME
This holds the wheels in place and gives the skate stiffness and control. It is usually made from aluminum or synthetic materials such as polycarbonate. Aggressive frames are fitted with additional grind plates.

Wheel frame — Litespeed (11.2 inches, or 285 mm)

LINER *(inner boot that fits around your foot)*
✳ Design — Liners are made from synthetic materials. They must fit well, and some even shape themselves to your feet! Look for ones with thick padding on the toes to help absorb hits.
✳ Hygiene — Liners can be removed from the shell. Aggressive skates usually have an antibacterial liner to reduce odors.

CLOSURE
In-line skates have different closure systems, including laces, zippers, Velcro straps, and buckles—sometimes all of the above!

Closure — Quick slide eyelets, lacelock, powerstrap, zip lace cover, and locking buckle

Micro-bearings

Wheels — 82 mm (3.2 in.)/ 82A Rollerblade LITE HP

WHEELS
Wheels come in different sizes and degrees of hardness. Standard wheels are 76 to 80 millimeters (3–3.15 in.) in diameter.
✳ Soft wheels give more grip and a softer, slower ride but also wear down quickly.
✳ Hard wheels last longer but give a more bumpy ride with less grip.

In-line for all

Whatever your style, there is an in-line skate for you. Not all skates are suitable for all uses, though, so choosing the right one is important. In general, you will get what you pay for.

Recreational skates

Standard recreational skates are the most common in-line skates, with lots of entry-level designs. They normally have all of the standard features shown on pages six and seven. They are good general-purpose skates for beginners to start with. Most can be upgraded with different wheels and bearings.

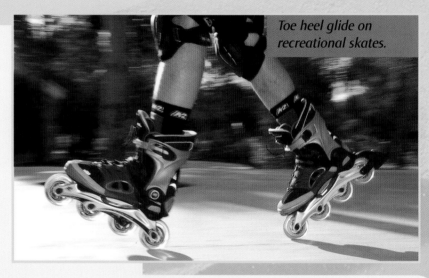

Toe heel glide on recreational skates.

Hockey skates

These have smaller, harder wheels to allow greater agility. Many of them are made with soft leather or synthetic shells. Better skates will have no liner and will use laces, rather than straps, as fastenings. Although hockey skates are great on rinks, they give a bumpy ride on general outdoor surfaces.

HOT HINT

"Try renting a few pairs before you buy. Some skate shops will even take the rental cost off the price of a new pair of skates. The main thing to remember is don't let yourself be pressured into buying skates that aren't right for you."
Jean Couderc, in-line skater from France

Hockey skates can be expensive. Many amateur in-line hockey players wear durable recreational skates like these instead.

Speed skates

Speed skates look very different from other in-line skates. They have a low-cut boot, which doesn't have a liner, and a longer wheel frame, with five instead of four wheels. They are very light and use materials such as aluminum or carbon fiber (lightweight but strong) for the wheel frame.

Speed skates are designed to be as lightweight as possible.

Aggressive skates

These skates are the in-line heavyweights—tough and virtually indestructible. They are specifically designed to take the serious hits and falls that are part of street skating. All aggressive skates have additional armor on the toe caps and around the ankles, and an extra-thick liner. They have four small wheels, usually about 55 millimeters (2.15 in.), that are protected by durable grind plates for serious rail slides (left). Most aggressive skaters customize their skates to fit their style.

Get geared up

In-line skating can be a dangerous sport—especially for beginners. It is important to have the right gear to protect yourself against injuries while looking cool, too.

Helmet

Your head is the most important part of your body. Even at slow speeds, a fall can cause serious damage, so get a helmet! You will find a variety to choose from depending on your skate style, but the most important thing is to make sure you get one that fits. Most helmets come with adjustable pads and straps.

Skating with friends. Learn from each other's experiences—especially when it comes to sharing safety tips.

HOT HINT

"Get a helmet! I mean it! You can break your arms or legs and still live. You don't want to break your head."
Tony Chen, skatefaq Web site

Body gear

As a beginning in-line skater, you should wear wrist guards (right), elbow pads, and kneepads (and a helmet). However, as you become more experienced, you may decide to wear only some of these. Buy the best quality gear you can afford—and make sure it fits. Poorly fitting gear offers you little protection and can be quite uncomfortable.

Be seen

If you are going to skate at night, make sure you can be seen by drivers, pedestrians, and bikers. To help you really stand out, wear bright-colored clothing, a reflective band around your arm or body, and skate lights.

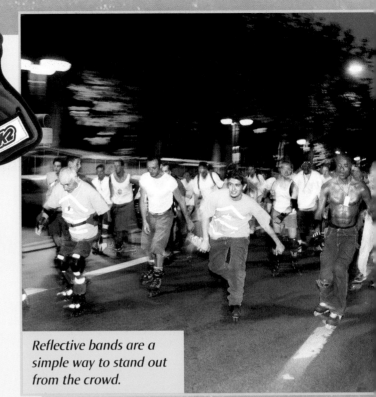

Reflective bands are a simple way to stand out from the crowd.

Hanging out at the skatepark. Some skaters say they don't wear a helmet because of the heat. Buy one that is a light color (to reflect the heat) or that has extra air vents.

Clothing

You can wear almost anything to in-line skate; it depends on your style. When starting out, long-sleeved tops and pants are best, as they offer extra protection when you fall—although they may not completely stop you from getting road rash! Most aggressive skaters wear loose-fitting clothing. Many recreational skaters wear clothing made of Lycra. In cold weather, fleece clothing and a sweatshirt can help keep you warm. A lightweight, waterproof jacket can protect you against the wind and rain.

HOT HINT

"Some people don't like wearing [body] gear. . . . It's up to you to stay safe. Whether you skate in a park or on the street, you should always wear wrist guards and a helmet."
Fernandez H. Sergio, Britain

Get ready to go

In-line skates are an extension of your body. They help you to glide along, but it's still your muscles that get you moving. Because of this, it is important to warm up first.

A good stretch

Stretching prepares your muscles for the activity you want them to do. A stretch should be a slow, gradual movement, not a sudden one. When you feel your muscles go tense, stop stretching and hold that position for about 15 seconds. Repeat each stretch several times, and make sure you do the same stretches on both sides of your body.

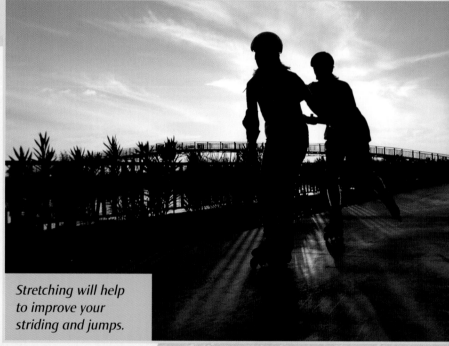

Stretching will help to improve your striding and jumps.

Hamstring stretch (left leg).

Hamstring muscle

Sit on the floor with both legs straight out in front of you. Bring one foot up toward your groin, but keep the other straight. Now slowly reach with both hands toward your farthest foot until you feel the tension in your hamstring.

Stomach muscles

The best way to exercise your stomach muscles (there are many) is to twist. Stand with your feet apart, and keep your body upright. Gently rotate your upper body at the waist (keeping your pelvis facing forward) until you feel tension in your stomach muscles. Then rotate to the other side.

Skate maintenance

Good skaters always make sure their skates are in good working order before they head out. Replace worn wheels or brakes, and lubricate any noisy bearings. Remember to take a repair kit and spares with you. And don't forget water and some snacks, too.

Twisting left and right helps to improve your flexibility and stomach strength.

HOT HINT

Do your skate maintenance at the end of a day's skating. That way, your skates are always ready to go when your friends call.

2.

3.

4.

5.

6.

1.

Repairs on the run:
If you are skating away from home, you should carry a few essential spares with you in a shoulder pack (1) or something similar. These should include a skate tool (2 and 3, normally supplied with your skates), some lubricant (4), and spare parts—bearings (5) and wheels (6).

Play it safe

In-line skating is exciting, but if you're not careful, a great day out can turn sour. Learning to play it safe can prevent such problems and make your experience more enjoyable.

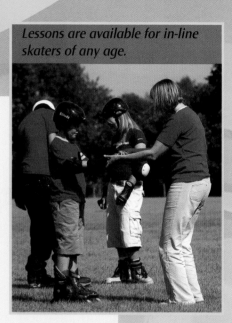
Lessons are available for in-line skaters of any age.

Look after yourself

Even with safety gear, you will fall. That's why it is always a good idea to try out your first moves on a soft surface, such as short grass. Take advice and lessons from more experienced skaters or instructors. This will help reduce the chance of sustaining a serious injury when you first start out.

You won't be performing like this on the halfpipe in your first session. Get to grips with the basics first.

When you are ready

Don't be pressured into doing in-line moves that you are not comfortable with. Remember, even the most experienced skaters were once newbies themselves! Becoming a really good in-line skater takes time, practice, confidence, and patience. You should only tackle new moves once you feel ready.

Watch the sun

Nothing beats cruising outside on a hot summer's day. The sun has hidden dangers, though, and can burn uncovered skin and dehydrate you very quickly. Wear sunblock or cover bare skin, and make sure you stop for regular water breaks. Sunglasses don't just make you look cool; they protect your eyes from the sun's glare, too.

Take time out to grab a snack and some juice. They will help to keep your energy level up.

Look ahead

With your new-found freedom, there is a temptation to go too fast too soon. It is important to make sure you can stop—just remember what happened to Joseph Merlin! Always look and think ahead, and slow down before you actually need to stop. This will prevent injuries caused by coming to an abrupt stop and will also make your brakes last longer.

Think of others

You must be responsible and think of those around you when you are in-line skating—a rude and dangerous skater gives all skaters a bad name. A skater traveling too fast in a busy place can be a scary sight. You should always give way to pedestrians and let them know you are coming—if they can't see you, simply say "pass please." If there are young children or animals where you are skating, you must take extra special care—they are sure to run out in front of you!

HOT HINT

"Watch out for sudden changes in the pavement surface. One minute, you can be striding along flat concrete, and the next, picking yourself up out of a hole!" Sunny Tobias, California

FROM THE EDGE

Safety tips for in-line street skaters:
* Always wear protective gear: a helmet, wrist guards, knee pads, and elbow pads.
* Learn in-line skating basics such as stopping and turning before going out.
* Stay away from water, oil, debris, or sand on the ground and uneven or broken pavement.
* Observe all traffic regulations.
* Move to the right of pedestrians, bikers, and other skaters to pass them.

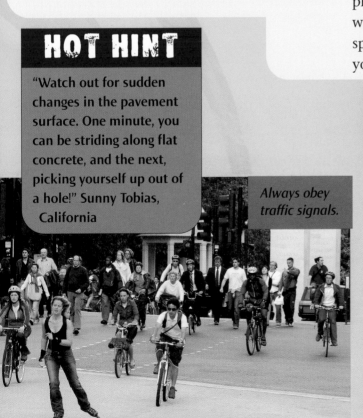

Always obey traffic signals.

Just For Fun

In-line skating is a competitive worldwide sport, but for the majority of skaters, it's simply a way to hang out and have fun.

Free Fun

Once you have purchased your basic gear, you can skate for free if you choose. Bike routes and local parks are particularly good places to skate, but some may not allow skating, so check first. Many towns are even building their own public skateparks to encourage skaters to stay off the streets.

Private session

Private skateparks have larger layouts than public ones, with ramps, bowls, and rails for you to practice on. They are a great place to meet and learn from more experienced skaters. You may have to pay to get in, but since many skateparks have areas set aside for beginners, it's worth spending the money.

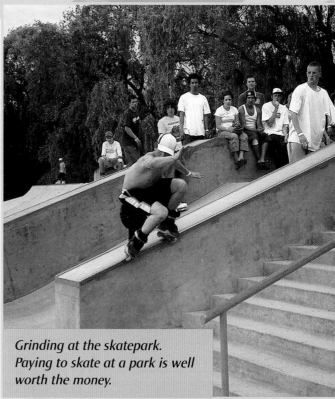

Grinding at the skatepark. Paying to skate at a park is well worth the money.

FROM THE EDGE

Many cities now have weekly meets where in-line skaters gather to socialize and skate. The "Pari-Roller" is the most famous of these skate meetings and takes place in Paris, France, where thousands of skaters meet for a late-night skate through the city. "France is the perfect destination for a skating vacation. It is the home of the world-famous Paris Friday Night Skate, which every skater should experience at least once in his or her life." Kathie Fry, editor of www.skatelog.com

FROM THE EDGE

In 1997, Zephyr Adventures (www.zephyradventures.com) was the first company in the world to organize trips for in-line skaters. People aged 11 to 72 take part in tours held in many places, including Florida, Germany, and Switzerland (right). "This skating trip rates as one of the best vacations I have ever had." Skater from the U.S.

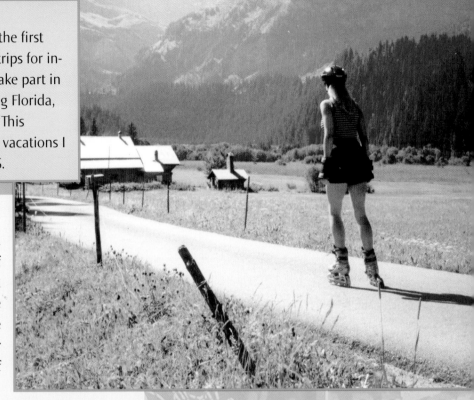

In-line experiences

In-line vacations and tours are a great way to get more out of skating and explore new places all over the world. You could explore Korea's volcanic Jeju island, skate through the heart of New York, or tour the rolling landscapes of Switzerland.

The Berlin skate marathon is the biggest in the world. In 2004, it was won by Roland Ehmann (men) and Stephanie Schubert (women).

In-line events

In-line events provide the perfect opportunity to meet other skaters, check out the latest fashions and gear, and take part in competitions. There are also skate marathons or half-marathons, which take place around the world from Germany to Tahiti. Skate magazines, shops, and Web sites usually advertise events, and there is almost certainly something happening near you.

In-line sports

Modern in-line skates were developed as a way to practice hockey. By 1995, in-line hockey had its own World Championship. Other sports, including soccer and basketball, soon followed.

In-line hockey

In-line hockey is one of the world's fastest-growing sports, with competitions at the local, national, and international levels. However, most in-line hockey is played locally in parks, gyms, or ice rinks. Each team has five players and must try to hit the puck into the other team's goal. The first-ever FIRS (International Roller Sports Federation) World In-line Hockey Championship was held in Chicago in 1995. It takes place in a different country every year. In 2002, the women's FIRS World Championship was held for the first time.

To the limit

FIRS was set up in 1925. It is the international governing body that incorporates both roller and in-line sports. FIRS works closely with the International Olympic Committee. Many people believe it will help to establish in-line hockey as an Olympic sport some day.

In-line hockey games are held on "plastic" and on the "street." They are fast and furious.

RollerSoccer

Back in 1995, Zack Phillips, an in-line skater from San Francisco, was skating when he kicked a soccer ball that crossed his path. He came up with a new idea, and within weeks, Zack was organizing the first in-line soccer matches with his friends. Each team had five players, and they created rules similar to soccer, but with some borrowed from in-line hockey, too. Today, RollerSoccer is spreading rapidly, with leagues in Britain, Pakistan, Brazil, and Australia, as well as across the U.S. In 2004, the RollerSoccer World Cup was held in London. The action-packed tournament was won by Germany.

FROM THE EDGE

"Players from a variety of sports backgrounds have been able to excel at RollerSoccer. Some of the best players could hardly skate when they started." RollerSoccer International Federation Web site (www.rollersoccer.com)

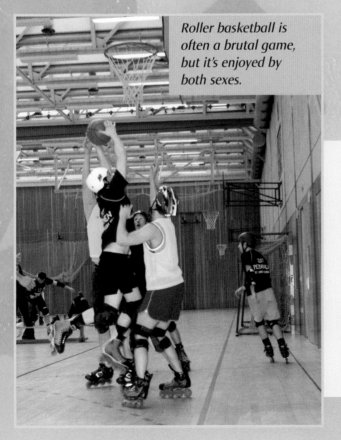

Roller basketball is often a brutal game, but it's enjoyed by both sexes.

Roller basketball

Basketball is already a fast and exciting sport, but add in-line skates, and the speed and thrills are doubled! American basketball player Tom LaGarde founded in-line basketball in 1992. It is centered around New York, where there are regular weekly games, but the sport has also spread to other American cities. Germany, the Netherlands, Pakistan, Brazil, and Portugal also have a growing number of players.

Basic skills

Most beginners are itching to get going, but it is well worth spending some time learning the basic skills. The best way to learn is to take lessons, but some basic starter skills will help you on your way.

Stay relaxed

Get used to standing on your skates before you try any moves—and stay relaxed! Stand upright with your feet shoulder-width apart and your knees slightly bent. Lean gently forward from your ankles onto the balls of your feet. Keep your shoulders relaxed and your head up, and stretch your arms out in front of you to help balance. This is the ready position. Practice this starting position until you feel comfortable.

HOT HINT

Don't forget to take a break. Just sit out of the action for 5 or 10 minutes every 30 minutes of skating—you'll find it easier to keep your energy level up.

First strides

1. From the ready position, bring your heels together and point your toes outward. You should now be on the inside edges of your skates in the "V" position.

2. Slowly roll one skate forward, and gently push off with the other. This pushing movement is called a stroke. As you make a stroke, move your weight forward onto the front skate.

3. As you move, lift the stroke skate (the back one) off the ground and glide forward. A stroke and glide together is a stride—the basic in-line move. As your stroke skate comes back to the ground, bring it parallel with your front skate and glide forward in the ready position.

Stopping

Stopping is the most important skill to learn. When gliding forward in the ready position, move your braking skate forward until its back wheel is level with the front wheel of the other skate. This is the scissor position. Lift the toe of your braking skate so the brake drags. Lean forward slightly at the waist and straighten your braking leg to increase the pressure on the braking skate. Keep your other leg bent at the knee until you come to a stop.

Moving on

Once you have mastered the basic skills, it is time to move on to some more advanced skills. These will allow you to begin serious in-line skating and are the starting point for learning in-line tricks.

Make that first turn

The first turn to learn is the "A-frame turn."

* Glide forward in the ready position, and allow your skates to move apart into an "A-frame."

* To turn, increase the pressure on one skate by pressing down with your toes and pointing the skate in the direction you wish to turn. If you put pressure on the left skate, you will turn right. Keep your body relaxed, and remember to look ahead. Complete the turn by bringing your feet back into the ready position.

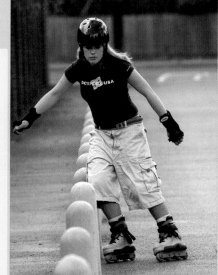

"Slaloming" around posts is a great way to practice turning.

Parallel turns are a more advanced way of turning. They help you to avoid trouble by turning quickly.

Parallel turns

To parallel turn, you need to glide with your skates in a narrow scissor position.

* Your lead (steering) skate will decide your turning direction. To turn left, your left skate should lead.

* Gently point your toes in the direction you wish to turn. This will put your skates onto their edges, ready to make the turn.

* Now, twist your body from the waist in the direction of the turn, and look where you are turning.

* Complete the turn by returning your body and knees back to the center.

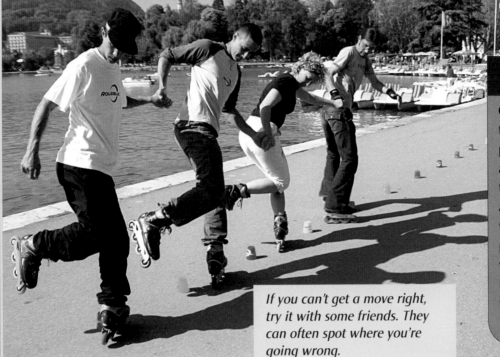

HOT HINT

Once you are confident, try putting several parallel turns together and learn to slalom. Try to vary the sharpness and speed of your turns, too. Mastering parallel turns will help you avoid obstacles and is one of the key moves for more advanced skills and tricks.

If you can't get a move right, try it with some friends. They can often spot where you're going wrong.

Stepping down

1. To go down large steps, it is best to stop and step down. But when you come to smaller, curb-height steps, you can slowly skate off of them. To do this, approach the step in a narrow scissor position and at a slight angle.

2. Keep your weight in the center of your skates, and just glide off. Your knees and ankles will cushion your landing, so keep them bent forward and relaxed.

HOT HINT

Hopping up a curb is trickier than stepping down. Practice hopping in place in your skates so you know you can get enough height before trying it for real.

Advanced tricks

Most tricks take a long time to master. It is a good idea to take lessons before attempting any of the tricks below.

Toe-heel glide

This is a fun trick that looks cool and can really improve your balance.
* Skate in a wide scissor position along a smooth surface. Tip your non-braking skate up so that you are gliding on its rear wheel.
* Point your braking skate so that you stand on the front wheel, or toe.
* Keep looking ahead, use your arms to balance, and keep your knees bent. This is a toe-heel glide. Start off slowly until you become confident.

Fabiola da Silva moving to Soul X Grind a halfpipe rail.

Grinding

Grinds are a big part of aggressive skating. The soul grind is considered one of the easier grinds—but there are lots of others to learn. To soul grind a rail:
* Get up some speed and jump up high enough to land on the rail.
* Land with both feet at the same time, with the outside of your back foot parallel with the rail (the soul position) and your front foot facing forward (frontside).
* Bend your back foot (or "soul" foot) to maintain your balance as you grind along the rail.

The jump

1. As you approach the ramp, you should be in the ready position, with your knees bent and your body leaning forward from the waist. You can push off the lip of the ramp to get extra height (air).

2. When you take off, pull your knees into your chest and swing your arms upward. This will help you get more air. To stay in control mid-jump, hold your knees up against your chest in a tuck position. As you exit the jump, lower your legs, keep your knees bent, and put your arms out in front of you.

3. Look ahead to where you are going to land, and start moving your feet into a scissor position. Your strongest leg should be at the rear. As your skates touch down, allow your legs to bend. They will help to absorb the impact. Once you have landed, you can safely return to the ready position.

FROM THE EDGE

"If you're just starting out, getting a nice tuck may be difficult. Keep working at it, though. It will really increase the height you achieve." Scott Weintraub, jumping tutorial at skatefaq Web site

HOT HINT

"Tricks are not just to show your skills, but are a good test of balance and will help further develop your all-around skating." Mark Heeley, author of *1st In-Line*

Get serious!

For most people, in-line skating is just a fun way to keep fit and spend time with friends. However, with ambition and a lot of determination, there are no limits to how far you can go.

Begin at home

In-line skating is a tough sport, and you need to be very fit and know enough tricks to really do well. Practice is the best way to make it to the top, so spend at least 30 minutes a day on your skates. Find out about clubs in your local area and join one. There you can improve your skills by watching others and sharing tips. Clubs also give you a chance to try different in-line activities so you can find out what style you enjoy the most.

Watching other, more experienced in-line skaters can give you ideas to develop your own moves and style.

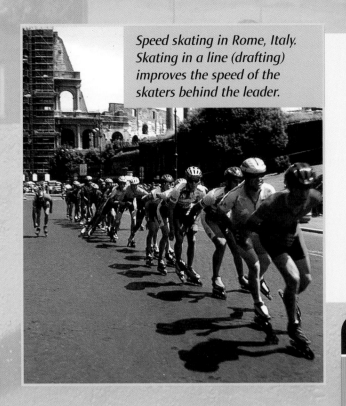

Speed skating in Rome, Italy. Skating in a line (drafting) improves the speed of the skaters behind the leader.

A world event

In-line skating is a world sport, and it's every serious skater's dream to appear in a world event. Start by entering local club competitions. All skaters start this way and then gradually begin to compete at regional, national, and international events. Another good way forward is to watch a major competition if it comes near your hometown. Not only is this a thrilling sight, but it's also a fantastic way to learn from the very best in the sport!

To the limit

The ultimate speed in-line skater is Theresa Cliff-Ryan. She has won 48 World Championship medals, including 25 golds—more than any other skater! Theresa started racing when she was just 15, winning three gold medals in her first year. She is one of the best in-line skaters of all time.

Go for gold!

At the moment, in-line skating is mainly limited to its own international events. In 1992, in-line hockey was a show sport at the Barcelona Olympics. It was very popular with the crowds, and there is hope that it will soon become an official Olympic event. In-line events, including hockey, speed skating, and figure skating, are already part of the Pan American Games. These games are held every four years and include the 42 nations of the Americas. The same in-line events were also part of the World Games in 2005. Maybe by the time you reach your best, in-line skating will be part of the Olympic Games—the world's biggest sporting event.

In-line events are held across the world and draw massive crowds.

Meet the pros

To become an in-line pro, you will have to put in lots of practice and be very determined. It is hard work, but if you make it, you will become a familiar name to thousands of fans.

Grabbing sponsorship

Sponsorship is a big deal—it helps great in-line skaters become stars by providing them with the best gear. Free goodies don't just fall from the sky, though. You have to earn them by being a great skater with a cool attitude. Once you've achieved a good position in local competitions, talk to the people at your local skate shop. They might give you some handouts and gear in exchange for putting their store's logo on your event jersey. Keep skating, and you just never know—maybe skate fans will be putting posters of you on their wall one day.

To the limit

RIDER PROFILE:

Fabiola da Silva of Brazil has appeared in 9 of the 10 X-Games (XG) events and has won 8 medals—7 of them gold! She is the best woman in the world at aggressive in-line and is now challenging the men, too. In the 2004 XG, she came sixth in the combined men's and women's aggressive in-line vert final.

To the limit

RIDER PROFILES:

Aggressive in-line skating is currently dominated by Japanese brothers Eito and Takeshi Yasutoko. Eito is the elder brother and the only male skater to have ever won three gold medals in the XG—in 1999, 2000, and 2003. He lost out in 2004 to his younger brother Takeshi, who added the gold to his five other XG medals. The members of the Yasutoko family are all skaters, and they have been nicknamed the "first skate family of Japan." They are known for trying exciting new tricks such as Eito's 1440 flat spin (four midair horizontal spins) and Takeshi's double Viking flip.

Takeshi Yasutoko's trademark double Viking flip has helped to build his skate style. Developing trademark tricks is just one way to get yourself noticed.

Members of the Canadian women's in-line hockey team celebrate their victory in 2004.

Hockey giants

The U.S. and Canada are the teams to beat in in-line hockey. In the 2004 FIRS World Championship, these two teams competed for the gold medal in both the men's and women's events. The U.S. men successfully defended their gold medal, but in the women's final, Canada beat the U.S. to claim the gold. The Czech Republic won the bronze for the women, and Italy claimed bronze for the men.

Jargon buster

ballistic nylon — a type of very tough plastic, used to make the shell of some in-line skates.

bearings — steel micro-balls enclosed within a ring that fits between a skate wheel and the axle; without them, the wheels would grind to a halt.

carbon fiber — a material added to skate shells to improve flexibility.

cuffs — strong, plastic ankle supports that help to transfer power from the legs to the skates.

durometer — a rating scale used to describe the hardness of plastic, ranging from 74A to 100A.

gliding — moving forward without pumping the legs.

grind plates — flat bars, usually made of tough plastic or metal, that are attached to aggressive skates to protect the frame and wheels and help grind.

grinding — moving along a rail or a curb; there are many different grinds.

FIRS — (International Roller Sports Federation) the in-line sports governing body.

frontside — a type of grind in which you jump clockwise onto an object with both feet positioned at 90 degrees to it.

halfpipe — a "U"-shaped ramp usually made of steel or wood.

Lycra — the brand name of an elastic fabric that is used to make sportswear.

newbie — a beginner or someone new to the in-line skating scene.

polycarbonate — a very strong plastic used to make in-line skate frames and other parts.

road rash — cuts usually sustained from scraping along the pavement after a fall.

slalom — the combination of several left and right parallel turns, one after the other.

sponsorship — when a skater is given money by an in-line team or manufacturer to race in return for promoting its products.

stride — the combination of a stroke and glide.

stroke — pushing off from one skate to the other.

X grind — a grind when both feet are "souling" from opposite sides (so you form an X).

vert — a halfpipe that becomes vertical at the top.

Find out more

Every effort has been made to ensure that these Web sites contain no inappropriate or offensive material. However, because of the nature of the Internet, it is impossible to guarantee that the contents of these sites will not be altered. We strongly advise that Internet access be supervised by a responsible adult.

www.aggressive.com

This Web site is packed with product reviews, trick and skill guides, links, photos, and a wealth of information to help you stay healthy and injury-free. It also has its own skater's log featuring music and games from the aggressive skating scene.

www.skatelog.com

Web site containing almost everything you need to know about in-line skating. Check out the guides, reviews, gallery, and many other topics to get you skating.

www.rollerskatingmuseum.com

The Web site of the National Museum of Roller Skating features on-line exhibits and history. The museum is committed to enriching the experience of all skaters.

www.k2skates.com

Up-to-date event reviews, in-line skating links, and athlete profiles—plus the latest skates, gear, and accessories from K2.

www.rollersoccer.com

Find out more about RollerSoccer on this Web site, which features the history of the game and plenty of hints and tips to get you started.

www.healthatoz.com/healthatoz/Atoz/hl/fit/spor/skating.jsp

Provides information about the health benefits of in-line skating.

www.rollerblade.com

Check out the latest skate designs, specifications, and tips on this Web site from the Rollerblade Corporation.

www.iisa.org

Web site for the International In-line Skating Association. It includes in-line skating news, skate care tips, and lots of information to help you buy the right skates and gear.

Index